Rockin' Crystals

How Healing Crystals Can
Rock Your Life

Also by Brenda DeHaan

The Craft Fair Vendor Guidebook: Ideas to Inspire

Crafty Decluttering

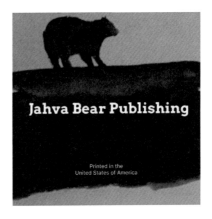

Jahva Bear Publishing

Printed in the
United States of America

Copyright 2018 by Jahva Bear Publishing
Text and photos copyrighted by Brenda DeHaan

First edition: August 2018

ISBN: 978-1-7180-8997-6

DeHaan, Brenda.
Rockin' Crystals: How Healing Crystals Can Rock Your Life
1. Crystal Healing.   2. Rocks and Minerals.   3. Holistic Healing.
4. Mind-Body-Spirit.   5. Inspiration and Personal Growth.

Dedication

This book is dedicated to

YOU, if you love crystals...

and to someone else, if you don't!

TABLE OF CONTENTS

Join me and see just how intriguing crystals can be....

Preface

When some people hear about crystal healing, they don't know what to think. Many people don't even *think* of crystal healing at all. I used to be one of those people.

Then my world changed. It improved, *and* it keeps getting better and better! After I experienced the healing properties of various crystals, I felt compelled to share my joy.

I took online classes through Hibiscus Moon Crystal Academy and became a Certified Crystal Healer in 2012. Even though I have a wonderful career being a school librarian, I still dreamed about opening a rock shop and doing crystal healing as my full time job. I live in a small town in South Dakota, so that wasn't very feasible--and I deeply value my librarian job. Outside of school, I started sharing my knowledge about crystals with interested people and have found a balance between working with crystals and my "day job." One sideline is wire-wrapping crystals and selling jewelry at shows and online. Even if people don't understand the healing possibilities of their jewelry, they are often still instinctively drawn to wear it.

I have learned a lot. I regularly feel like I am getting younger, not older. I am extremely happy with my life, and crystals have become part of who I am.

A friend's nephew stopped at my house when traveling through town. He lives in the Black Hills; we had never met before. He looked around at my displayed crystals and kindly said, "So you are one of those people who stops at the rock shops in the Black Hills. I always wondered who actually stops at those places."

You bet, I stop there! In fact, I lose myself and find myself in those rock shops. I love them!

When many people think of crystals, they think of only clear quartz. This stone may be "crystal clear" or look like lead crystal glass, and it may be called rock crystal, but clear quartz is just one of thousands of crystals. When I use the term *crystals* in this book, I mean a multitude of rocks, stones, and gemstones that have a fixed geometric structure and are made naturally. I am calling them *crystals* in the generic sense.

crystals:
healing stones,
many colors
(not glass)

I believe that God created crystals as one avenue of natural healing similar to herbs, essential oils, and other remedies inspired by nature. Also, *healing* and *curing* may be synonyms, but they can signify quite different results. One interpretation is that healing encompasses a broader scope that includes spiritual, emotional, or energetic shifts whereas curing implies more of a physical recovery from an illness.

Rockin' Crystals is the story of my journey told in a down-to-earth manner. It answers many questions that I am commonly asked when talking with people about healing crystals.

Why I am sharing this? I have been an English teacher and school librarian throughout my adult life, so I automatically want to help people find information and answers. So if you are curious about crystals, this book is for you!

How It Started

My journey with crystals started literally and figuratively in 2010 on a road trip with my sister Liz and friend Gwenna to the Rocky Mountains. We stayed in a cabin at Estes Park. Shopping included visiting some rocks shops. I had never spent any time in a rock shop, but I'd always wanted to stop at some when visiting the Black Hills. My husband never wanted to stop at them, though, and I didn't insist (back then).

While at our first rock shop in Estes Park, I browsed in the various rooms and then went outside to join Gwenna while my sister continued to look.

"I kind of got a headache when I was in the rock shop, but I feel fine now," I mentioned to my friend.

Gwenna explained that rock shops give her headaches because of the stones' vibrational energy, so she went outside. I did not understand how this worked, but I had a slight buzzing in my head that demonstrated that she knew what she was talking about. We went into numerous rock shops. My head would soon tingle; when I'd leave the rock shop, the pressure would evaporate.

If not sensitive to crystalline energy, one would not feel that head buzzing. It does go away after becoming acclimated to the crystals' vibrational energy.

During our stay at Estes Park, I bought my first three crystals: a tiger's eye, a clear quartz, and a chevron amethyst. These stones were just the beginning of my adventurous voyage. Who knew that a road trip could transform one's entire world view? It's not that I lost my former outlook or beliefs, but I added another layer of understanding about the natural world.

my first 3 crystals in 2010

CLEAR QUARTZ

tiger's eye   chevron amethyst

lapis lazuli earrings

In a crystal healing book for sale in one store, I read about how lapis lazuli supports the immune system. I was struggling with rosacea at the time, so I bought some lapis lazuli earrings while at Estes Park. I wore the earrings frequently and kept the tumbled tiger's eye, amethyst, and clear quartz in my pockets but didn't think much about it. The large tumbled crystals were like palm stones in a more natural shape. (A palm stone is a smooth, symmetrical stone that fits well in your palm; people rub them to calm themselves or "just because." They are comforting.)

Fast forward to March 2011 when my husband, daughter, and I went to the Black Hills to celebrate Easter with my in-laws. I visited a rock shop and bought two pink rhodonite necklaces (for more autoimmune assistance) and a large fluorite that reminded me of an Easter egg. I routinely wore the rhodonite necklaces and added the fluorite to my pocket.

I had bought three books on crystal healing and would read them periodically. I was aware that different stones were recommended for various ailments and emotions, but I didn't believe that crystals would initiate any dramatic changes in *my* life. I was just interested in the possibilities. Boy, was I ever surprised when things started happening!

Weight Loss

(Now this subject got your attention, didn't it?!)

By Memorial Day weekend 2011, I noticed that I had lost seven pounds. The *only* thing I'd changed was carrying stones in my pockets every day.

"Do you think carrying rocks in my pockets could have caused me to lose weight?" I asked my husband.

"I don't know. Maybe they improved your metabolism somehow," he replied. It seemed like the only explanation available since my eating and exercise had not changed at all.

I had lost 18 pounds by April 2012 and have kept most of it off since then. The only other time I'd lost weight before was when I'd gotten divorced years before, and that was a miserable way to lose weight!

It seemed too good to be true, but it really happened! I had (and still have) more than 18 pounds to lose; the crystals' energy took me only so far. The rest remains up to me with diet and exercise, which hasn't been too motivating! So I carry some extra weight and am continually grateful that I lost weight and kept it off.

Another bonus: By April 2012, my triglycerides had dropped 91 points. As of July 2018, they were the best they have been since I first had my triglycerides tested over 10 years ago.

Before sharing more examples of improvements in my life facilitated by crystals, I would like to mention some aspects of energy that you may not have considered before.

Energy & Chakras

Everything is some form of energy. We are made of energy and have energy fields surrounding us. This includes crystals which oscillate with a steady vibration.

Think about a time when you felt like someone behind you was staring at you. You turn around, and, sure enough, someone is looking at you intently. When they see you looking back at them, they might smile, wave, or quickly look away. It depends on why they were looking at you. However, *how did you know* someone behind you was looking at you in the first place? You felt that person's energy going out to you.

Here's another example of energy. You work for hours doing something that does not involve much physical labor. You have to concentrate for an extended period to accomplish your task. You may have to get other people to do things that they don't care about doing. At the end of the day, you are exhausted! This job took a lot of energy, even if you didn't burn many calories physically. Emotional, mental, and physical energies use different forms of energetic output. Emotional and mental energy can drain your physical energy; conversely, doing something physical can boost your mind and emotions.

You can feel your own energy by rubbing your hands together briskly. Then hold them a few inches apart with the palms facing each other. Sit quietly and see how long it takes to start feeling any tingling emanating from your hands. You can also do this with a partner where you hold your palms 2-3 inches apart from each other. It may take several minutes to feel the energy.

We don't normally notice someone else's energy, but it's still there. Just because we don't feel different forms of energy doesn't mean that these energies don't exist. Although most humans can't feel WiFi energy in a building, a cell phone and laptop can easily detect these waves. Machines and people are "wired" differently, of course, but some people can feel the EMF's (electromagnetic frequencies). Stones such as black tourmaline, shungite, hematite, and amazonite can help protect you from EMF's.

Humans and other living beings have subtle etheric energy fields more commonly known as auras. Most people cannot see auras, but science has advanced to the point where machines can photograph auras and chakras.

Our bodies have spinning wheels of energy known as *chakras* (a Sanskrit word for "wheel" or "circle."). We are essentially human grids with many wheels of spinning energy. Seven main chakras reside along the spine. Not only that, we have an inner rainbow associated with these seven chakras.

Red - root chakra at base of the spine

Orange - sacral chakra

Yellow - solar plexus chakra

Green - heart chakra

Blue - throat chakra

Indigo - third eye or brow chakra

Violet - crown chakra

Ideally, our energy should rotate in a clockwise motion from head to toe to be at our peak. You can imagine how often humans remain at their ideal peaks! Crystals can help us with this goal.

My first experience with a "rainbow boost" was after a colonoscopy. (Oh, joy!) Afterwards, I felt sad and out-of-sorts...still "wonky" from the anesthesia. I had an idea to put a rainbow of crystals in my pockets (seven crystals, one for each rainbow color); within 20 minutes, I felt "normal" again. The crystals reset and balanced my chakras and improved my mood. It was wonderful!

Then I learned how to do a crystal layout on myself to balance my chakras. Although only a rainbow of stones is needed, I usually add a black stone or two at my feet and a clear quartz above the crown chakra. The black is to keep me grounded via "earth star" energy; the clear quartz is to enhance my connection to universal energy. As stated earlier, we have many chakras in addition to the "rainbow 7." Each stone's

vibrational energy and color frequency correlate well with the chakra's natural color in a way to easily balance your own energy.

At some holistic shows I sold crystal chakra kits and included the instructions below. Each kit contained seven crystals, one from each color in the rainbow.

RAINBOW CRYSTAL LAYOUT

* Wear comfortable clothing and lie down someplace peaceful and relaxing. Place crystals on the designated chakras listed in the order below.

*ROOT CHAKRA: Place a RED crystal near the base of the spine/pelvic region.

*SACRAL CHAKRA: Place an ORANGE crystal approximately 2" below your navel.

*SOLAR PLEXUS CHAKRA: Place a YELLOW crystal 2" above your navel.

*HEART CHAKRA: Place a GREEN crystal between the breasts.

*THROAT CHAKRA: Place a LIGHT BLUE crystal on your throat.

*THIRD EYE CHAKRA: Place an INDIGO crystal on the middle of your forehead.

*CROWN CHAKRA: Place a VIOLET crystal just above your head.

Lie quietly with crystals in place. Concentrate on your breathing. Envision each color of the rainbow filling your body one color at a time.

After 20-30 minutes, remove crystals from the crown on down, leaving the red a few extra minutes for grounding. Cleanse your crystals after each layout. *(More on cleansing later.)* Feel relaxed and refreshed!

****

Crystal layouts can vary to fit various purposes; they're not for only chakra balancing. It is important to have your chakras balanced, though, because this balance affects so many areas. Other types of layouts are also beneficial.

If you are feeling emotional or unloved, rose quartz would be a fitting crystal to use in your layout. Clear quartz could also be added to amplify the rose quartz's healing properties. Crystals that assist with grief issues include rose quartz, amethyst, and Apache Tears. Sodalite decreases anxiety and increases intuition. Emotions impact our physical health, and crystals can support emotional healing.

rose quartz...
master healer
for emotions &
all types of love

When I attend holistic health fairs, I have my aura picture taken at a fellow vendor's booth, Sacred Designs by Spirit. I put my hand on a special aura reading machine, and it somehow takes pictures of my aura and chakras. Since life is never constant, my aura fluctuates as well.

On the picture below, notice how inconsistent my chakras were on that day. If my energy would have been balanced, the chakras would have been approximately the same size and would have rounded, smooth edges.

My heart chakra was huge in the picture. It seems like it would be a good thing to have a big heart, but that's not the case in the world of chakra balancing. My heart chakra was so off-kilter because this photo was taken two days after we had to put our 3-year-old dog Rex to sleep because of a

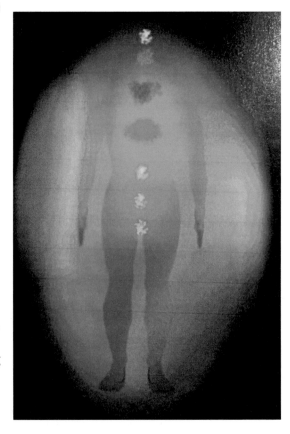

brain tumor. I was grieving; my heart hurt.

While sitting at the aura reading booth, I grabbed a beautiful clear quartz wand.

"Look at this wand!" I exclaimed.

Shimen, the talented woman who can see auras even without her machine, said, "You should see how your aura changes when you hold it! In fact, I'll take a picture and show you."

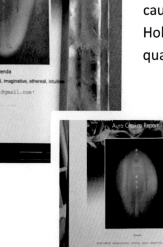

My chakra colors became more uniform in size, and my overall aura color changed. What caused the change? Holding that clear quartz wand!

My chakras were more balanced a year later, and my overall aura was "blue-indigo" again.

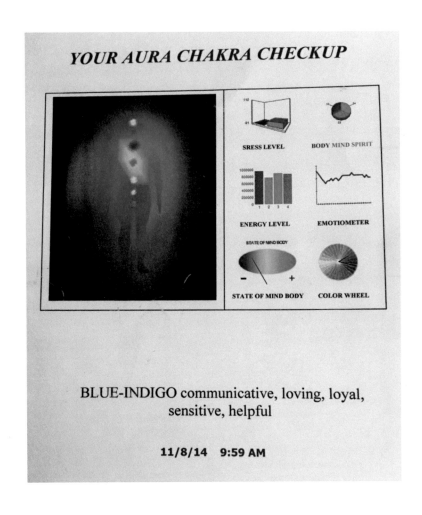

YOUR AURA CHAKRA CHECKUP

BLUE-INDIGO communicative, loving, loyal, sensitive, helpful

11/8/14   9:59 AM

In 2017, my aura was deep green.

YOUR AURA CHAKRA CHECKUP

SRESS LEVEL   BODY MIND SPIF

ENERGY LEVEL   EMOTIOMETEI

STATE OF MIND BODY   COLOR WHEEL

Brenda

DEEP GREEN balanced, social, teacher, love peopl
nature, animals

11/4/17   12:54 PM

This 2018 chakra checkup contained a nice mix of aura colors with the main aura color as deep green again. I was a vendor at a holistic health show and visited some neighboring booths. Another vendor who sold only shungite invited me to hold two large shungite rods for 15-20 minutes and feel the energies. I visited the aura photo booth not long afterwards, and I think the shungite affected my colorful aura balance.

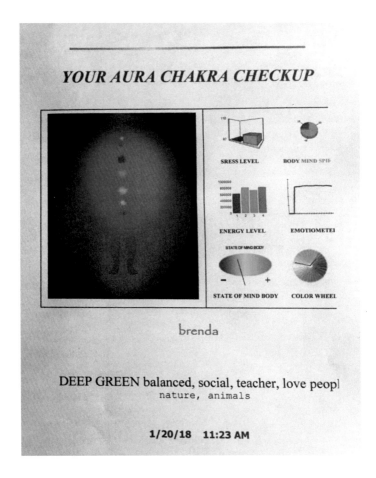

YOUR AURA CHAKRA CHECKUP

brenda

DEEP GREEN balanced, social, teacher, love peopl
nature, animals

1/20/18   11:23 AM

Having the science and technology capable of documenting phenomena like this gives a visual component to the energies usually not seen. Generally, in the physical world, seeing is believing; in the metaphysical world, *not* seeing is often still believing. Naturally, it's easier to believe when we can see or feel something. Crystals are physical objects that can stimulate metaphysical changes. These are difficult to prove, but science and technology are gradually making it easier.

Crystal structures have a solid, fixed geometry, and the stones are millions (or billions) of years old. Crystals have a steady energy emanating from them. The mineral composition and color frequencies also influence their energies.

People, on the other hand, are comprised of a lot of fluid and soft tissue and have fluctuating energies. Illness, stress, injury, or exhaustion can get energy fields out of balance. Doing a crystal layout, carrying rocks in your pockets, wearing crystal jewelry, or just having them nearby can help. The crystals act as a tuning fork and reset a person's energies back into a better pattern or rhythm.

Another analogy is to think of when a radio station is just one digit away from being on the correct frequency; for example, 107.2 instead of 107.3. You may still hear the station, but it's full of static. One click over, and the music is clear. Likewise, the crystals can help a clearer frequency flow through you. It's not that you wouldn't heal without the crystals, but they can enhance the process, speed, or depth.

Skeptics may say that crystals heal due to the placebo effect. Well, if that's the case, so be it. Improvement is improvement.

Faith is a part of people's belief systems. I have faith that crystals improve my life, but if others don't believe, that's fine. Live and let live!

More on Energy

Not everyone can feel a stone's energy, but the techniques below may help. Before trying either one, rub or lightly clap your hands together to stimulate those nerve endings and energies. Are you ready?

1. Hold the crystal in your palm, sit quietly, and see if you feel any sort of tingling in your hand.

2. Hold your fingers curved over the stone and see if you feel any tingling in your fingers.

If you do not feel any type of physical sensation, that's OK. It may take multiple attempts, or it might not work for you. Just because you can't feel the energy doesn't mean that it's not there...but it *is* more reassuring if you can feel an energetic "charge."

Having more physical energy is another benefit that I have noticed. Before carrying crystals in my pockets, I would feel so fatigued by the end of work that even walking to the car seemed daunting. Now I feel a "reasonable" amount of tiredness at the end of the work day. I almost always carry a red jasper and an orange carnelian in my pockets at work. I refuse to buy pants without pockets, which limits my wardrobe. If you don't have pockets, wear crystal jewelry. I also wear a lanyard I made with clear quartz and black tourmaline for my work ID badge.

Every once in a while, I forget to put rocks in my pockets before going to work. My lanyard and crystal jewelry are always there, though! I started making wire-wrapped jewelry in November 2011 and almost always wear my own jewelry, each piece of which has at least one healing crystal.

How do I decide which crystals to carry or which jewelry to wear? Intuition matters more than anything else. I see which ones catch my eye and go from there.

Rarely can I carry just one type of crystal at a time, even though focusing on one or two is the standard recommendation. My instincts urge me to put a variety in my pockets. I prefer the same number of stones in each front pocket.

I currently own over 40 books on healing crystals, including a few that are more about the rocks' and minerals' geological traits (which aren't nearly as much fun for me). I can't remember the details, especially when so many crystals exist. If I am looking for something specific to work on, yes, I will use the books for reference or will search online. Otherwise, I go with my intuition.

The Internet offers thousands of sources of information regarding crystals from websites to YouTube videos to social media groups. Just search for "healing properties of blue lace agate" (or whatever stone interests you) or "healing crystals for insomnia" (or whatever ailment or condition you'd like information about). Look at multiple results to compare information and go with what sounds right for you.

I live in a rural area where people know a fair amount about each other's hobbies and interests. I was asked to give presentations about rocks to first and second grade classes. Before talking to any class, I explained my crystals background with the administration.

I showed the students different specimens of rocks and the contrast between tumbled and rough stones as part of their science State Content Standards. South Dakota also adopted the Oceti Sakowin Essential Understandings and Standards (Native American State

Content Standards) to be taught. Stones have been a holistic aspect of Native American culture for thousands of years, and I did several rock presentations in middle school and high school science classes.

At school, I am a librarian 100% and share the physical, geographical aspects of rocks with students. If the older students have heard about and ask about a stone's metaphysical properties, I tell them that I don't discuss healing properties at school, but a huge amount of information is available online. Because some people view crystal healing as controversial, I keep clear boundaries between being a public school librarian and being a Certified Crystal Healer.

Another staff member told me a few years ago that a second grader had said, "When I grow up, I am going to be a librarian who collects rocks like Mrs. DeHaan!" Kids are instinctively drawn to rocks, so they appreciate seeing my collection.

Sometimes when I am introducing crystal healing to individuals at home or at a holistic health show, I will display an array of crystals and ask which one appeals to them the most. After they pick, I have them read about the selected stone's properties and ask if it applies to their lives. So far, *yes* has been the answer every time. I use books that give condensed, basic information because the more in-depth ones can be overwhelming at first.

In fact, even I with my crystals background may still feel "information overload." I refer to my crystals books regularly, but I skip around all over the books to whichever sections are relevant to the moment.

With thousands of crystals available, one way to simplify is to focus on the seven basic chakra colors and find stones in the color zone correlating with your situation. Then expand as you feel more knowledgeable.

Earth Energy

Crystals can be all around you without you even realizing it. You may interact with them without realizing it also.

A very informal kind of crystal layout is when you "lay out" on the beach. Quartz is composed of silicon dioxide; a common element of sand is silicon dioxide. Sand also may be made from bits of feldspar and other minerals. When you lie on the beach, you benefit from the sand's crystalline energy, the earth's energy below, and the sun's energy shining down. These make a great combo to make you feel great!

In fact, you don't have to lie down to receive energy from sand and rocks. If you live in a cold climate, a warm day in March may tempt you to head to the beach and feel the sand (and maybe some icy water) on your feet. Being outside surrounded by nature perks spirits and perspectives. Being barefoot "grounds" you.

37

Crystals at Work and Home...Magical!

Without realizing it, most people have crystals working in their homes and businesses: quartz clocks and watches, quartz computer chips, LCD (Liquid *Crystal* Display) screens, telephone and microphone speakers, and more. Crystals are used in medical equipment like ultrasounds and laser lights.

Many people regularly eat crystals: halite, more commonly called "salt." Pink Himalayan salt is becoming more available, even in small towns. Some people use pink Himalayan salt lamps to cleanse the room's energies or to add ambiance, some eat this salt by using a grinder, and some like having both. The regular white salt is also a crystal.

Clear quartz has piezoelectric qualities (produces a charge under pressure) and oscillates at a constant rate of over 32,000 vibrations per second. That steady beat is why quartz works so well in watches, clocks, and various electronic devices. Scientists have figured out how to make synthetic versions of crystals to use in machines and components as well. This is all beyond my scope, but I mention it to promote awareness of crystals' technological uses.

An "aha" moment for me during a crystals class session was the point that what some call *magic* could still be "real" science but without the technology advanced enough (yet) to document it. For instance, someone 100 years ago would have viewed walking on the moon, microwave ovens, the Internet, and cell phones as magic. Today's technology still seems like magic to me, but some people actually do understand the science behind it all.

Wands

Wands are a different type of crystal tool. Depending on their shapes, they may be used to direct energy through a point or may be used as a massage or reflexology tool. They might have one pointed and one rounded end, two pointed ends, two rounded ends, or naturally

formed ends. Reflexology may be done on the ears, hands, or feet.

Caution: Do **NOT** use a wand for reflexology or massage if pregnant. You do not want to inadvertently trigger an unintended reaction that could cause premature labor or some other complication.

natural clear quartz wands

wands on agate slice

EnVISION More Healing

I first needed glasses in fourth grade and have worn them or contacts ever since. My glasses require a high degree of correction as well as several prisms in the lenses to keep my eyes aligned. I also had a vitreal detachment in one eye. I am old enough to require trifocals, and I have dry eye syndrome. I need my glasses to do anything and everything (except sleep, of course).

I started having double vision in 2012, so my eye doctor fit me into his schedule right away.

I told him, "Maybe my vision has improved, and my glasses are just too strong."

He just stared at me like I was a total dreamer, paused and said, "Yes, wouldn't that be nice? And I would be *very* happy for you if that were the case."

After examining my eyes, he seemed stunned and said, "You're right!"

My right eye had improved "3 grades," and my left eye had improved "2 grades." I don't have the optical background to explain this better, but this is a large improvement in the world of glasses.

I asked him, "Do you want to know *why* my eyes improved?"

Of course, he wanted to know! I assumed that a medical doctor would be skeptical about crystal healing. Nonetheless, my optometrist knew my eyes, and he'd seen the improvements with his own eyes...and with the medical equipment that had documented those improvements.

"I am taking online classes to be a Certified Crystal Healer. Ulexite is supposed to help with vision, so I have been sleeping with ulexite underneath my pillow," I explained. "The crystals' vibrations help get our bodies' energies back into sync."

I needed to order new glasses ($800). That $1 ulexite was pretty expensive in the long run but well worth it!

Before I left, my eye doctor said sincerely, "Thank you for the information."

Every visit since then, we have been curious to see any vision changes. Overall, I have had numerous small improvements. Twice I needed stronger bifocals, but then later needed weaker bifocals. Twice I needed nothing changed at all. Most recently, my vision improved where I needed new glasses in December 2017 and then new glasses again in July 2018. Using crystals associated with vision certainly seems to be helping me.

Regarding the dry eye syndrome, at first I needed to take four Dry Eye Omega supplements nightly and use eye drops. It didn't take long before I needed to take only two supplements (half the recommended dose) and no longer needed any eye drops.

Ulexite

I slept with just one dime-sized ulexite underneath my pillow for approximately six months before having that interesting eye appointment where my eyes had dramatically improved.

It is also known as the "TV stone" because of its resemblances to a TV's fiber optic qualities. The parallel fibers transmit light. Ulexite may be thick, but you can still read through the clearer ones. Do not rinse them with water because that can make them cloudy.

Ulexite is inexpensive; the saying, "You get what you pay for" does NOT apply to ulexite. It's a budget-friendly stone that had a big payoff for me. I have often seen ulexite selling for only $1 for a small piece.

The new lenses have been costly, but I am just so happy to have improved vision. I have kept the same frames for four years, so that helps financially.

I stopped putting crystals underneath my pillow because my dog kept jumping onto the bed and searching for them. She would put them in her mouth; I would have to get them back. (Animals are attracted to the energy of crystals and respond to their healing properties also.)

Finally, I had the idea of placing my glasses onto two large slabs of ulexite while I slept. Do the metal frames absorb the ulexite's vibrations? I don't know; I do know that my eyesight keeps improving.

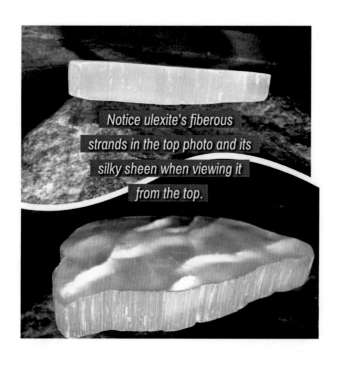

Notice ulexite's fiberous strands in the top photo and its silky sheen when viewing it from the top.

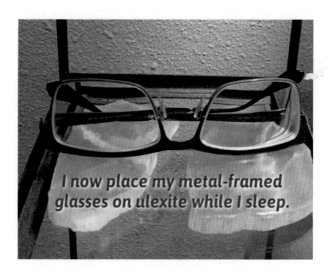

I now place my metal-framed glasses on ulexite while I sleep.

Eye Agates and More

Stones with an eye "signature" (natural eye design) are also reputed to assist with the eyes.

THIS AGATE RESEMBLES *a brown eye so much that* IT FREAKS OUT SOME PEOPLE!

Can you see the owl design?

49

Green-eyed malachite?

Green garnet an "eyeful" of beauty!

Night Vision

Tiger's eye is associated with improved night vision.

This tiger's eye reminds me of a car.

After reading that tiger's eye helps with night vision, I bring a tiger's eye with me whenever I know that I will be driving at night. I bought one tiger's eye that resembles a car, but I usually leave that one displayed in a vintage printer's letterpress tray.

If I will be out of town overnight, I like to bring a rainbow of crystals with me. My yellow chakra choice is often a tiger's eye. When traveling with a rainbow, I know that I will have what I need to keep my energies balanced.

Abundance

What do you think of when you hear the word *abundance*? Does it have a positive or negative meaning? I think of *abundance* as having plenty of what I would like, especially regarding money. However, you need to be very precise in what you want when you try to attract abundance because who wants an abundance of troubles?

Back when I was dreaming of opening a rock shop and was still taking classes to become certified as a crystal healer, I participated in a meditation activity to attract abundance. Later that week, I had a 324-mile trip to Sturgis that had already been rescheduled once. A lapidary/rock auction was being held that same weekend in Yankton on the opposite side of the state.

I asked my husband to go to the auction for me. Neither of us had been to a lapidary auction before, and he knew next to nothing about crystals. I wish I could have gone to it, but he did an incredible job. I came home to *abundance!* My crystals collection went from modest to *whoa, baby!*

Most of the people bidding were there for the lapidary equipment and rocks that they could cut and polish. They weren't interested in the small tumbled stones, so my husband brought home a lovely abundance.

Some of the specimens were in their natural rough state. I didn't know what many of the stones were at that time, but I researched what I could. Some were labelled, which really helped. I have one book, *The Crystal Healer* by Philip Permutt, which arranges stones by colors. If you do not know where to begin figuring out what a certain stone is, searching the appropriate color section is one way to start.

A few years later, another lapidary auction was held in the area. The July heat was overbearing, I have had heat exhaustion before and can't tolerate much heat, but I was *not* going to miss this auction! The elderly seller had collected most of the rocks himself, including an impressive collection of Fairburn agates, South Dakota's state gemstone. (Rose quartz is the state mineral.) The choice Fairburn agate was bigger than a golf ball and went for over $400. I was shocked!

People came from the Black Hills and all over to this auction, so I was afraid that I wouldn't be able to afford much. Most of the bidders appeared to be interested in the larger and/or more collectible stones. I'm sure that I was the only one there to buy stones for their healing properties and to expand my wire-wrapping jewelry business. Score some more abundance! (I would have done cartwheels, but I didn't want to hurt myself!)

Prairie agates may be found in the Kadoka, South Dakota, area. I haven't searched for any there, but I sure like the ones I bought at the auction!

It's a good thing the wavellite was labelled.

Azurite and malachite often grow together.

I was thrilled to get the rough Apache Tears (black with white) and rough and tumbled amethyst points, but the auction containers had to go!

The auction pictures are just samples of what I won. Lapidary auctions are not common in my state, but I wish they were!

I have purchased crystals at rock shops in the Black Hills, at holistic healing shows, at flea markets, online, and wherever I can find them. Most of the rocks shops in the Black Hills are open only during the summer tourist season, but some remain open year round. We have relatives in the Black Hills; during one of my visits, I went to nine rock shops in one weekend. I lose all sense of time in two places: rock shops and public libraries. I usually have to visit these by myself.

With rock shops, not every store carries the same stones. Some are higher priced on some varieties and quite reasonable on the others; different stores may be the reverse. With time, I have learned which South Dakota shops offer the best prices for certain crystals. With thousands of crystals in creation, no one store can carry everything. Granted, the common crystals are in most stores, but I couldn't believe it when one rock shop did not have any green aventurine. To me, that was a basic stone that would be in every business that sold crystals.

Here are some Black Hills rock shop purchases.

I have ordered from eBay and have had good results overall. It's obviously better to see and hold the rocks before buying them, but that's not always feasible, depending on how close you live to rock shops and shows.

I think amethyst is a popular crystal that most people buy when starting their own collections. I view amethyst as the "gateway crystal." It attracts people's attention and encourages them to start buying crystals. It's considered the #2 master healer with clear quartz as #1. Amethyst is a form of quartz.

The "cathedrals" are the large, usually dome-shaped geodes that can weigh tons. This one is a statement piece in a jewelry store in Spirit Lake, Iowa. The picture does not show its true beauty.

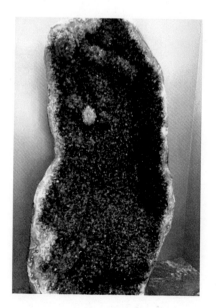

More home decor stores and magazines are starting to feature crystals as decorations. Crystals do add a soothing ambiance to each room where displayed. They can calm emotions and relax people overall. People cannot see the crystal vibrations, but they often feel them and may linger in rooms with lots of crystals.

Dyed Crystals

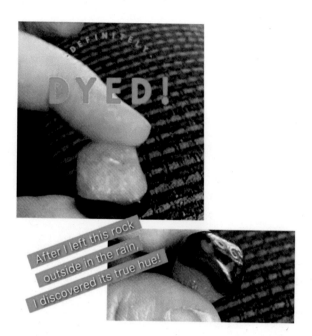

When I first started my collection, I filled little velvety bags of colorful rocks from souvenir shops. I didn't realize that a percentage of them were dyed. One time I put them on the painted deck railing to get a natural cleansing from the rain. Surprise, surprise! Probably ⅓ of them lost their vibrant colors and deposited dye residue on my tan deck railing. They were natural stones, just not natural colors!

I have read that dying doesn't change a stone's healing properties, but the key is to know what the original stone is. Magnesite and howlite absorb dye very well. If you see something that says, "Turquoise howlite," that is not real turquoise. It is turquoise-COLORED howlite. Technically, a turquoise-colored stone may be called "turquoise" because of its color, so don't automatically assume that it's genuine turquoise stone, especially if it's inexpensive.

If you love turquoise, research it in books or online to learn what to look for and what to look out for! I have written blogs for Turquoise Skies, www.tskies.com, about the metaphysical aspects of turquoise, and they publish other types of blogs that explain many details about turquoise. The company specializes in turquoise jewelry made by Native Americans in the Southwest, and their blogs are very informative.

The top picture shows all genuine turquoise. The beads in the plastic container are mainly reconstituted turquoise (like turquoise dust or scraps with added resins, etc.) They work for jewelry but not for healing. The person bead is dyed howlite; the chunk on "his" left and the chunky earrings are dyed magnesite. I didn't understand about dyed magnesite at the time, but the "person" bead was labelled as dyed howlite.

Agate slices are commonly dyed when made into coasters and night lights, for example. I have seen geodes dyed deep purple, fuchsia, turquoise, and other colors. If the outside of the geode is colored a lighter shade than the color inside instead of looking like a grayish rock, it has probably been dyed. Some stones are vibrantly hued naturally, but many of the deeply colored ones are dyed or heat-treated. I prefer natural colors, but if you like the dyed stones, that's fine. It really is. Just be conscious of what you are buying if something seems deceptive, underpriced, or overpriced.

amethyst geode

(not dyed)

The dyed green stone below is one of my favorites because of the design my friend Gwenna noticed when she held the back side up to the light. I don't know how or why it happened so artistically, but it is a special stone to me.

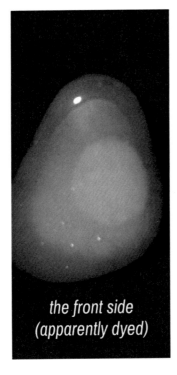

the front side
(apparently dyed)

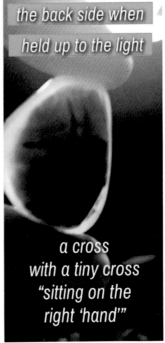

the back side when
held up to the light

a cross
with a tiny cross
"sitting on the
right 'hand'"

Crosses

People have requested that if I see anything else with crosses (like my dyed surprise) to buy it for them. I have told them that they need to find those types of stones themselves because if I find them, I am keeping them!

Cracks filled with other minerals can create natural cross shapes like in this carnelian.

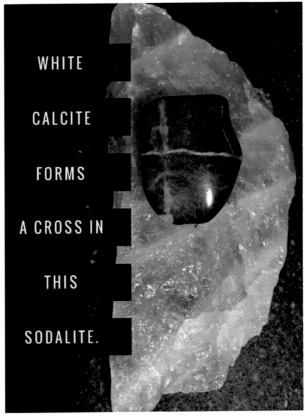

WHITE

CALCITE

FORMS

A CROSS IN

THIS

SODALITE.

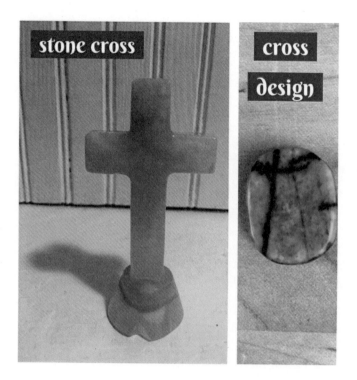

A cross is challenging to carve because of the intersection of both horizontal and vertical lines. I used to make a lot of cross necklaces but quit because some broke if handled too much. One teenage boy put his cross necklace in his pocket to play basketball. Snap!

People have no idea how fragile a rock can be. Some stones crack or break without very much pressure or friction.

I bought hand-carved crosses labeled as onyx, which I interpreted to mean as a harder stone, 6.5 - 7 (out of 10) on the Mohs hardness scale. I also thought of onyx as a black stone.

After some crosses broke, I researched online and realized that this so-called onyx was called Mexican onyx, which may be calcite (Mohs 3) or aragonite (Mohs 3.5 - 4). Because of its softness, Mexican onyx works well for carving animals, turtles, wine goblets, and other objects. Mexican onyx is quite different from "regular" onyx.

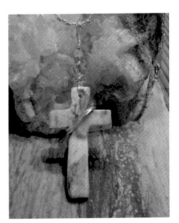

For cross necklaces now, I use either hematite (Mohs 5 - 6), thicker stones, or add semi-precious gemstone beads to a metal cross.

Other Popular Shapes

Hearts are often a desired motif, both carved and natural.

hearts, carved and naturally (irregularly) shaped

This heart-shaped clear quartz geode looks like a laughing face!

crazy lace agate:
two sides, two hearts

aquamarine

Botswana agate

smokey quartz (with rainbows)

Who can resist a ?

Whether in the ground or in our homes, stones emit energy and may change in appearance. For instance, many of my crystals have developed rainbows. The longer I have had some of them, the more rainbows have appeared. My clear quartz wand was mainly clear, but a few months later, it had become cloudy. At first, I really worried about it. Then I noticed that my clear and smokey quartz cloud up if I hold or carry them a lot. I now view this change as an energy ex*change*. Crystal occlusions remind me of the clouds needed before seeing the rainbows, just like seeing a rainbow after a storm outside.

80

Angels and Their Wings

Cleansing and Charging Crystals

In order to maximize a crystal's healing energy, it needs to be cleansed and recharged periodically. Think of it as a sponge that absorbs to its saturation point and needs to be refreshed.

I used to cleanse my crystals monthly with the full moon, but after I had accumulated an abundance of crystals, it wasn't realistic to do this. If I use crystals on a layout with someone, in a grid, or carry them a lot, then I cleanse them; otherwise, it's random, depending on when it occurs to me.

The methods below may be employed in general, but these are mere guidelines:

★ Rinse the stone under flowing water. (The sink faucet is fine, but you need to make sure that your crystal isn't water soluble or toxic. Research this online.) Envision any unbeneficial energies going down the drain and back into the earth to be neutralized. Set the intention for the crystal's energy to serve for the highest good with grace and ease.

★ Use a tuning fork set to a frequency programmed to cleanse crystals. (Mine is 4096 Hz.)

★ Place crystals alongside or on top of selenite. Carnelian is also supposed to help with cleansing.

★ Place the crystals inside a container of brown rice.

★ Bury the crystal in the ground. (Remember where!)

★ Smudge with palo santo wood, sage, cedar, or sweet grass. If the smoke bothers you, sage and other sprays are available.

★ Surround the crystals with flowers or flower petals.

★ Place the crystal in rock salt. Some crystals are too fragile for this.

★ Place crystals outside in the rain or snow for a natural cleansing, but you don't want to put a warm, room-temperature crystal outside if the weather is really cold because the contrasting temperatures could cause cracking.

★ Play really loud music to "reset" the vibrations.

★ To recharge, put crystals outside or on a window sill during a full or new moon.

★ Some crystals may be put in the sunshine, but colored quartzes like rose quartz, citrine, and amethyst can fade if left in the sunlight too long.

A clear quartz sphere can even start a fire if the sunlight directs a beam of light too intensely.

★ Play a crystal singing bowl.

★ Your intentions are huge. You could breathe on a crystal and set your intentions to cleanse and/or charge. The mind offers powerful energy, so combine it with crystalline energy.

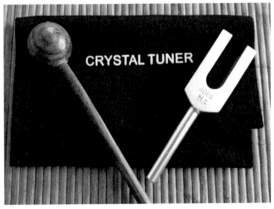

Your Glorious Instincts

Which crystals should you ᴜ

you put in your pockets? Which crystal ʲᵉ

wear? What does each crystal do? Is it going tᴏ

How do you know?

Listen to your intuition! Try to not overthink; just follow those intuitive instincts. Deep inside, we *do* know what is best for us.

Silently ask yourself a question and go with the first answer that pops into your mind. That's your inner guide, so let it guide you!

If you feel drawn to buy a certain crystal but have no idea why, buy it. Later, something may arise where it will suddenly make sense to you why you wanted that certain type of crystal, even though it seemed a mystery at the time of purchase.

One way to deepen your intuition is to meditate. Listen to guided meditations on YouTube; they offer a vast array of topics. Pick whatever fits your mood, listen, and relax! Search for about any topic, and you will most likely find a pleasing selection.

Your Special Space

Crystals add a calming, uplifting vibe to your home. If possible, create a special space where you can display your crystals, meditate, and just relax and rejuvenate yourself. If you don't have enough "room for a room," then designate a corner of a room as yours.

Having a spot where you can connect with your crystals by looking at them closely, watching how the light reflects, or focusing on other details is a way to forget stress and stay mindful in the moment. Schedule quiet time for yourself to decompress and let your mind float. It takes time and personal space to revitalize yourself, but it is so necessary for your entire well-being

The screen porch of my 1930 home was converted into an enclosed front porch long before I bought the house. I transformed it into my reading nook with two recliners. I have an amethyst mini Biomat and a Biobelt on one recliner. The crystals inside these devices heat and provide infrared heat and healing. I relinquish this relaxing spot to my guests, but I start and end my day on my Biomat recliner. It's my peaceful place.

In addition to relaxing on my Biomat, I often put large rose quartz stones on my shoulders while I read. They look goofy but feel marvelous! My jaws used to pop and crack so much from TMJ. Now it is rare for this to happen. I give the rose quartz the credit for relaxing my jaw, neck, and shoulder area.

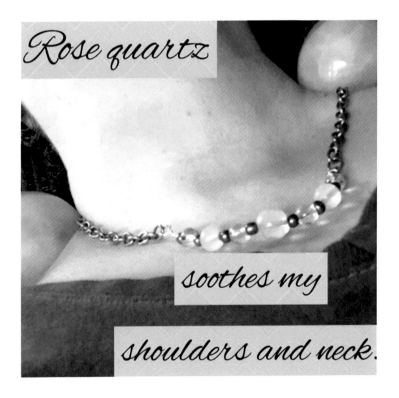

Rose quartz soothes my shoulders and neck.

Crystals are in almost every room in the house, and I sell them also. My reading room has the best collection, and those are not for sale.

Some of my favorites reside right next to my recliner.

Special larger crystals include a 21" tall amethyst, dendritic rose quartz, naturally heart-shaped quartz geode, and a rare mountain dendritic agate that I can't remember the exact name of, which is frustrating! I hate it when I am "sure" that I will remember the name and then later forget!

(Dendrites appear when iron and manganese fill cracks; they look like ferns or other plant life.)

I was blessed to purchase two huge quartz clusters from a massage therapist friend. She asked only for what she had paid for them 30 years ago. Inflation was not factored in because she wanted them to go to someone who would cherish them, and she wanted her money back but no profit. She said that she had shared their energy and beauty for 30 years and that was payment enough.

They are stationed underneath my grandparents' antique pie safe because they are quite sharp, and I have young grandchildren. The one on the right side weighs approximately 50 pounds. The one on the left weighs much less but cost twice as much because it is double terminated (crystals growing on both sides). To move them, I wear gloves to avoid cutting my hands. A folded rug protects the wood floor. I can see and admire them from my recliner.

Quartz is a common crystal around the world. That is very fortunate because clear quartz is considered the top crystal healer of them all. It can be programmed for an immense variety of intentions, and it amplifies the energies of other nearby crystals.

Colored quartz varieties include amethyst, rose quartz, citrine, aventurine, carnelian, and more. Colors vary depending on the earth's natural irradiation and/or the minerals melded with the quartz.

Storing and Displaying Crystals

The bigger your rock collection, the bigger the space needed. Another consideration is storing them in a manner where they aren't likely to get scratched or broken. I haven't done a good job with keeping crystals separated because I have so many. It's a wonderful problem, I know! To have some semblance of order so that I can find what I am looking for, I have sorted by color. Almost every room in the house has crystals somewhere. My reading room has the most, and it's where I spend most of my leisure time. I started with one small bowl of crystals; then I expanded to a mesh-wire silverware tray.

Now I have a cabinet with glass pedestal bowls of crystals for sale, a large jewelry box with two colors per drawer for personal use, and crystals on shelves and on tables and all over the place. With crystals, less is never

more, and hoarding is totally understandable, even admired!

The four drawers in my jewelry box contain rock jewels: red and orange in drawer #1, yellow and green in drawer #2, blue and purple in drawer #3, and clear/white, and black in drawer #4. Pink used to be in the bottom drawer also, but then I accumulated enough pink to need a larger space. As you can see, I have a wide variety of "pocket rocks."

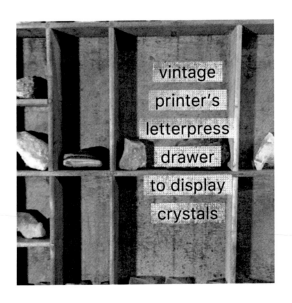

vintage printer's letterpress drawer to display crystals

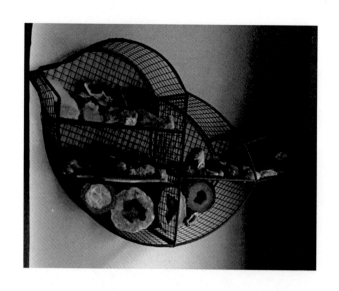

Rough and Tumbled

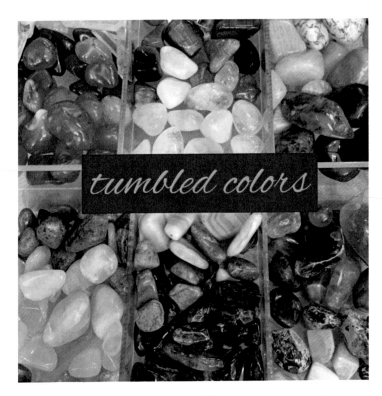

It takes weeks of tumbling to turn rough or raw stones into glossy tumbled stones. I have never done it; I have just heard about the process. If I were a rock hound and found my own stones, then I would tumble them to see the changes.

Some people feel that the energy is stronger and more pure if the stone is in its rough state. I cannot tell the difference, but people have diverse ability levels when it comes to discerning energy.

I prefer the smoothness of the tumbled stones, but that doesn't mean that I don't also appreciate the rough stones. I love them all!

TIP: Group tumbled stones together and place raw stones in separate sections or containers so the rough ones don't scratch the smoother stones. Plastic fishing tackle boxes have handy storage dividers.

Gem quality stones are obviously much more expensive than the same variety used for healing. Most of the gems used in fine jewelry nowadays are heat-treated to deepen the colors. They are tiny compared to most healing crystals.

I have always loved jewelry and used to value the precious gemstones much more than semiprecious. I didn't realize the energetic value of the semiprecious gemstones, but I do now! If the raw ruby (below) would have been gem quality, then I would not have been able to afford it. Part of the beauty of healing crystals is that they are affordable and beautiful.

ruby:
healing crystal
"wearing" a
gem quality ruby ring

Grids

If one crystal has energy, that impact can be amplified by using multiple stones to create a grid. Crystalline teamwork!

To create a grid, you may use special designs based on sacred geometry, such as the "flower of life" (pictured) or other geometrical patterns, especially those in nature. You can use your intuition and make your own pattern.

Normally, you have a larger stone in the middle of the grid with a balanced array of crystals radiating out from and/or around the center stone. You might want to write down your special intention underneath the center stone or grid.

I have created grids for other people and grids for myself. To respect the recipients' privacy, I am not going to explain the details but will share photos of some grids. They depict how grid patterns can vary and do not need to be perfect. Your intention is the key factor. It's difficult to "prove" how much a grid helps, but I believe in its energetic assistance and have seen positive results.

My Catholic friend Cami told me that saying the rosary is a form of meditation for her. She often says the rosary for other people's benefits. I am not Catholic, but I can see the resemblances of saying the rosary for a special intention and creating a crystal grid for a desired outcome.

A grid can be a visual form of prayer. Grids radiate a lot of combined energy that travels unseen through the universe.

I prefer making my own design with crystals that have associated qualities with the grid's projected intention. I tend to use rose quartz regularly because it is so helpful with emotions and the heart chakra. Other common themes for my grids include chakras and crosses.

love and peace

Finding a spot for your grid where other people won't touch it can be a challenge. It's natural for people to ask about the compelling pattern out of rocks because they are not used to seeing things like that.

If
searching
for direction
in
life,
use
any
stones
to
make
an
arrow
pointing
north.

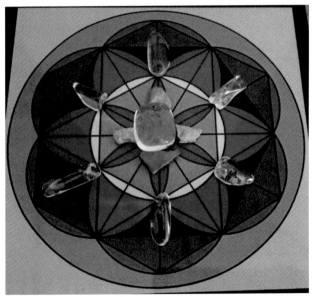

You can grid your home, office, or yard. Black stones are known for protection. One option is to put almost any black stone in the four corners of your room, home, or property to create an energetic grid of protection. Suggested stones are Apache Tear or black tourmaline. Apache Tear is a softer form of obsidian. Regular black obsidian should be used for only 20-30 minutes at a time because its energy can be overwhelming and can bring you down emotionally. If gridding your house and yard, bury the stones in the four corners of your land's property lines. They can remain there forever.

With a smaller grid created for a special intention, keep it in place until you feel like it doesn't need to be set up any longer. (Intuition!) Then cleanse the stones. Depending on the moon cycle, I may or may not charge them. I might just put them away and let them rest and recharge themselves. I will not use the gridded crystals again for a long time. (I have lots of crystal options.)

When using crystals, one suggestion is to say a prayer for pure goodness and light with God's highest blessings for all who have ever come into contact with the crystals and for all who ever will.

Enjoy!

This book is a sampling of anecdotes about crystals and how you may use them to enhance your life. Testimonials pique interest, but just because something works for one person doesn't guarantee that every other person will have the same results. Commonalities do exist, though. The more you learn about crystals and their healing properties, the more you'll know what should work for you.

In short, have fun with crystals! Let them lighten your life in ways best suited for your situation. Life has twists, turns, and unrouted detours, and that's what keeps it so interesting. Explore and flow forward!

Embrace your intuition and continue reading and learning. If the interest in crystals is there, pursue it! Whether this book is the beginning of your crystal quest or if you are already on your way, I truly wish you the best. Enjoy your journey and keep rockin'!

For Further Exploration...

The titles listed in this section are my ever-growing personal library on books about healing crystals, rocks and minerals, and energy. Although authors may agree on various metaphysical points, people have different experiences, trainings, and perspectives. There is no one perfect answer, solution, or proof. Not everything works the same way for everybody in so many of life's situations. We must each find our own way. Books can help.

So much of the universe is not understood yet. Of what *has* been discovered and explained, how much do most people fully comprehend? We have so very much more to uncover and learn! Quantum physics, metaphysics, "regular" physics...they're all ultra-complex.

My life has been improved by learning about metaphysical qualities of healing crystals. I am not an expert and never will be, but I hope I have provided some insight into your own crystal journey. This book's information contains the best of my current knowledge; any mistakes were unintentional.

If interested in learning more, explore some titles listed below. I leave it to you to discover which books resonate the most during this time in your life. NOTE: The European authors' books are also available in the US book markets.

Askinosie, Heather. *Crystal Muse: Everyday Rituals to Tune in to the Real You.* Carlsbad, CA: Hay House, 2017.

Brzys, Karen A., Thomas P. Shearer, and Candace Prill. *Agates: Inside Out.* Gitche Gumee Agate and History Museum, 2010.

Campbell, Dan. *Edgar Cayce on the Power of Color, Stones, and Crystals.* New York: Grand Central Publishing, 1989.

Emoto, Masaru, and David A. Thayne. *The Hidden Messages in Water.* Beyond Words Publishing ; London, 2005.

Gienger, Michael. *Healing Crystals First Aid Manual - a Practical A to Z of Common Ailments.* Forres, Scotland: Findhorn Press, 2006.

Gienger, Michael, and Joachim Goebel. *Gem Water: How to Prepare and Use More than 130 Crystal Waters for Therapeutic Treatments.* Forres, Scotland: Earthdancer Books, 2008.

Gienger, Michael, and Chinwendu Uzodike. *Healing Crystals: The A-Z Guide to 555 Gemstones.* Forres, Scotland: Earthdancer, 2014.

Gienger, Michael. *Gemstone Healing - How to Choose and Use the Right Crystal and Healing Tech.* Forres, Scotland: Findhorn Press, 2014.

Gienger, Michael. *Twelve Essential Healing Crystals: Your First Aid Manual for Preventing and Treating Common Ailments from Allergies to Toothache.* Forres, Scotland: Earthdancer GmbH, and Imprint of Findhorn Press, 2014.

Gienger, Michael, and Astrid Mick. *Crystal Power, Crystal Healing.* London: Cassell Illustrated, 2015.

Grey, Aruna Dawn. *The Stones Speak.* 2011.

The Group of 5. *Crystals and Stones: A Complete Guide to Their Healing Properties.* Montreal, Canada: Paume De Saint-Germain Pub., 2010.

Hall, Judy. *The Crystal Bible.* Godsfield Press (Great Britain)/Walking Stick Press (Cincinnati, OH), 2003.

Hall, Judy. *The Crystal Bible 2.* Godsfield Press (Great Britain)/Walking Stick Press (Cincinnati, OH), 2009.

Hall, Judy. *Crystal Healing.* London, Great Britain: Godsfield Press, 2011.

Hall, Judy. *101 Power Crystals: The Ultimate Guide to Magical Crystals, Gems, and Stones for Healing and Transformation.* Beverly, MA: Fair Winds Press, 2011.

Hall, Judy. *The Encyclopedia of Crystals.* Beverley, MA: Fair Winds, 2013.

Hall, Judy. *Crystals for Psychic Self-protection.* Carlsbad, CA: Hay House, 2014.

Hall, Judy H. *Crystal Prescriptions - the A-z Guide to over 1,250 Conditions and Their Ne.* John Hunt Publishing, 2014.

Hall, Judy. *Crystal Prescriptions: The A-Z Guide to over 1,200 Symptoms and Their Healing Crystals*. Ropley: O Books, 2006.

Kircher, Nora. *Gemstone Reflexology*. Rochester, VT: Healing Arts Press, 2006.

Lambert, Mary. *Crystal Energy: 150 Ways to Bring Success, Love, Health, and Harmony into Your Life*. New York: Sterling Pub., 2005.

Lanning, Nicole. *Practical Crystal Healing: 555 Tips & Techniques*. Bloomington, IN: CreateSpace, 2009.

Leavy, Ashley. *Crystals for Energy Healing: A Practical Sourcebook of 100 Crystals*. Beverly, MA: Fair Winds, 2017.

Lembo, Margaret Ann. *The Essential Guide to Crystals, Minerals and Stones*. Woodbury, MN: Llewellyn Worldwide, 2013.

Lilly, Simon. *Healing with Crystals: A Concise Guide to Using Crystals for Health, Harmony and Happiness*. London: Southwater, 2001.

Lilly, Sue, Michelle Garrett, and John Freeman. *Crystals, Colour & Chakra: Healing and Harmony for Body, Spirit and Home: Learn to Harness the Transforming Power of Natural Energies with Practical New Age Techniques and over 1000 Stunning Photographs and Artworks*. Lorenz Books, 2007.

Magnuson, James. *Fairburn Agate of the Black Hills*. Adventure Publications, 2012.

Melody. *Love Is in the Earth: The Crystal and Mineral Encyclopedia: The Liite Fantastic: The Last Testament*. Earth-Love Pub. House, 2008.

Mason, Henry M. *The Seven Secrets of Crystal Talismans: How to Use Their Power for Attraction, Protection & Transformation*. Woodbury, MN: Llewellyn Publications, 2008.

Mason, Henry M. *Crystal Grids: How to Combine & Focus Crystal Energies to Enhance Your Life*. Woodbury, MN: Llewellyn Publications, 2016.

Mégemont, Florence. *The Metaphysical Book of Gems and Crystals*. Rochester, VT: Healing Arts Press, 2008.

Mitchell, Krista N. *Change Your Energy: Healing Crystals for Health, Wealth, Love & Luck*. New York: Sterling Ethos, 2016.

Moon, Hibiscus. *Crystal Grids: How and Why They Work: A Science-based, Yet Practical Guide*. Charleston, SC: CreateSpace, 2011.

Navran, Shakti Carola. *Jewelry & Gems for Self-Discover: Choosing Gemstones That Delight the Eye & Strengthen the Soul*, Woodbury, MN: Llewellyn Publications, 2008.

Permutt, Philip. *The Complete Guide to Crystal Chakra Healing: Energy Medicine for Mind, Body, and Spirit*. London: Cico, 2009.

Permutt, Philip. *The Complete Guide to Crystal Chakra Healing: Energy Medicine for Mind, Body, and Spirit*. London: Cico, 2009.

Permutt, Philip. *The Crystal Healer: Crystal Prescriptions That Will Change Your Life Forever*. London: CICO Books, 2016.

Peschek-Böhmer, Flora, and Gisela Schreiber. *Healing Crystals and Gemstones: From Amethyst to Zircon*. Old Saybrook, CT: Konecky & Konecky, 2003.

Rosen, Brenda. *Crystal Basics: How to Use Crystals for Wellbeing and Spiritual Harmony*. London: Hamlyn, 2007.

Scott, Martin J., and Gael Mariani. *Crystal Healing for Animals*. Forres, Scotland: Findhorn Press, 2002.

Silveira, Isabel. *Quartz Crystals: A Guide to Identifying Quartz Crystals and Their Healing Properties*. Forres, Scotland: Earthdancer, 2008.

Simmons, Robert. *The Pocket Book of Stones: Who They Are and What They Teach*. Berkeley, CA: North Atlantic Books, 2011.

Simmons, Robert, Naisha Ahsian, and Hazel Raven. *The Book of Stones: Who They Are & What They Teach*. East Montpelier, VT: Heaven & Earth Publishing, 2015.

Symes, R. F., R. R. Harding, and Paul D. Taylor. *Rocks, Fossils & Gems*. New York: DK Pub., 1997.

Symes, R. F., and R. R. Harding. *Crystal & Gem*. New York: DK Publishing, 2004.

Virtue, Doreen, and Judith Lukomski. *Crystal Therapy: How to Heal and Empower Your Life with Crystal Energy*. Carlsbad, CA: Hay House, 2009.

About the Author

Brenda DeHaan has Iowa roots but ended up being transplanted to South Dakota. She is a wife, mother, and grandma who loves to read and write (and eat chocolate). You already know how she feels about crystals!

She would like to thank Jennifer Poncelet for her dedicated proofreading assistance and valuable outlook and Shimen Phelps Averhoff for her uplifting input and ongoing inspiration.

To contact the author, you may message her through her Etsy store, www.rockincrystals.etsy.com, or through her Rockin' Crystals Facebook page.

For more information about amethyst Biomats, see the products page at https://rockincrystals.biomatnetwork.com.

Made in the USA
Lexington, KY
10 August 2018